SUPERHUMAN
EYE CONTACT:
How to Radiate Confidence, Attract Others, and Demand Respect... With Just Your Eyes

By Patrick King
Social Interaction and Conversation
Coach
www.PatrickKingConsulting.com

Table of Contents

Introduction

My first real job interview was when I was 20. I had just finished my sophomore year of college and was looking for a summer job.

It was an exciting time, and during the period I was applying, the world looked like my oyster.

Endless possibilities with endless potential. I saw the path to becoming a CEO flash before my eyes.

What if I could work at so-and-so prestigious company? Oh, but what if this other Fortune 500 company gave me an offer first? Wait, what if this world-renowned professor calls me back first and wants to negotiate something for the summer?

It didn't really occur to me that I would have to first nail a bunch of interviews to have that luxury of choice... and objectively speaking, I was terrible in interviews. My credentials and grades were great, but I'm sure the same could be said for most of the applicants.

So what was going to set me apart?

My first interview was for the aforementioned Fortune 500 company and was an unmitigated disaster. I spilled coffee on myself, and then the interviewer's desk. I stumbled over my answers, and over the carpet on the way out. I did not get a second round interview.

My second interview was for the unnamed prestigious company that was based in New York. It was an improvement, and I almost made it out with my dignity unscathed. Unfortunately, I managed to break the interviewer's framed picture of his grandfather on his office bookshelf. I did not hear back from them.

My last hope for my summer of endless potential was the interview with the world-renowned professor. He had pioneered some psychological terms that were actually household terms, so this would be an amazing resume boost if I could land it. Plus, we were born in the same small town – didn't I have this in the bag?

Obviously not.

This time, no major mishaps that one could deem a party foul occurred during the interview, and I actually had a good gut feeling as I left his laboratory. Of course, I didn't hear back for a third time and was resigned to working as a lifeguard for the summer as I had done in my early teens. Prestigious, indeed.

What happened?

I thought I was eminently qualified, but I had just struck out and my self-esteem was at an all-time low. I told my dad about what had happened and he encouraged me to reach out to my interviewers for feedback in the hopes of improving my chances for next summer.

So I reached out and it turned out that my interview skills were fine, but that my general people skills were lacking. Specifically, I acted like I was afraid of making eye contact with people, which tends to give off serious "creep" and "shifty" vibes. It just makes people uncomfortable, which is the last thing you want to do when talking to someone... especially when they are determining if they want to spend significant time with you. My other interview failures probably weren't related to my proclivity to break objects.

For strangers, dating, friends, co-workers, eye contact is a key facet of what makes people like and respect you. It can even be a huge part of why you either get the guy/girl or don't.

All of this from eye contact? You better believe it. Think of how many of the idioms in English are based on characterizing someone's eyes.

Shifty eyes. Bedroom eyes. The Evil Eye. Kind eyes. Knowing eyes. Dead eyes. It's no coincidence.

Let's turn your eye contact superhuman and upgrade your respect, confidence, and life!

Chapter 1. Why is eye contact so important?

It doesn't matter whether the following is true or not because people believe it... and that's why eye contact is so important.

People impart so much meaning and importance to people's eyes that if your eye contact is lacking, you simply fall into the pit of negative adjectives.

People whole-heartedly believe that the eyes don't lie.

They believe that they can see people's character through their eyes, and a single look can determine trustworthiness and worth. It's one of the keystones of determining whether someone is lying. People use it as their north star – their guiding light on how to read you, and what kind of person you actually are.

Is all this fuss true and valid?

It's debatable... but if people believe it, it might as well be true for your purposes. In other words, it's not a battle you can win and you should upgrade your eye contact.

Eye contact is quite important if your goal is making a strong and powerful impression.

So what does superhuman eye contact make people think about you?

All the good things in life.

That you're confident, powerful, and typically get what you want.

That you aren't passive, have strong character, and are highly competent.

That you are trustworthy and loyal.

But let's be clear that you don't even have to have superhuman eye contact for people to assume those traits about you. Simply having decent or passable eye contact is the bare minimum for them. This means that you can't be *bad* at eye contact... or people will assume the worst, like they did the best if they saw your superhuman gaze.

What does someone with below average eye contact get labeled as?

Creepy, untrustworthy, and of weak character.

Strange, uncomfortable, shifty, and suspicious.

Yes, really.

You have to admit that when you meet someone that scans the room behind you and constantly avoids eye contact that you think that there is something simply odd about them.

Aside from our laymen perception, it's also something that has been scientifically proven.

One of the biggest signs that physicians look for in diagnosing infants with autism (or any number of afflictions on the autism spectrum) is a lack of meaningful eye contact. It turns out that eye contact is a hallmark of both social and mental development. It's a biological necessity for connection and relationships.

Eye contact is a biological and evolutionary imperative for our development as a functional human being. Not much more needs to be said.

As I said before, simply being competent with eye contact will afford you many of those benefits, but our goal isn't just to be competent, is it?

Chapter 2. Why is superhuman eye contact so difficult?

For even the best public speakers and coaches, superhuman eye contact isn't something that they were just born with.

It was a process, and something that only came about after a certain degree of self-awareness, comfort zone destruction, and hard work.

If you meet someone with great or even intimidating eye contact, it's highly likely that they have spent time drilling their eye contact through uncomfortable situations to improve.

Society is indirect.

Most societies simply aren't raised realizing the value of eye contact. In fact, many Eastern countries actually place little emphasis on eye contact because it can be seen as confrontational, argumentative, or disrespectful.

Western countries may place some value on eye contact, but Western society is a construction of politeness and manners, where being too direct and straightforward in general is off-putting.

In other words, most societies are roundabout and indirect by nature. This means that eye contact, something that is inherently brazen and direct, isn't something that we're used to. And it's something that we are increasingly less exposed to because of the way our modern digital and electronic age has evolved.

Emphasis on other skills.

Another reason that we are typically terrible at eye contact is that we don't learn the soft skills like we do academic skills.

But when's the last time you used calculus, and how often can you use eye contact to make a great impression on someone?

When you don't learn the basics of eye contact, it becomes a bad habit that is too easy to fall into.

This is the trap of the resume versus the personality. People like to emphasize the hard skills that you can list on a resume, but neglect the skills that will simply make you a more likable person and actually get you the job.

Shyness and anxiety.

Of course, for many others that have issues with eye contact, it's a shyness and anxiety issue.

Looking someone directly in the eye without wavering can be an intense feeling, and there's a tension that builds up instantly. It's this tension that we wish to avoid because we don't know what to do with it, so we often react in ways that are awkward or uncharacteristic.

We feel like it's too bold and forward, and draws undue attention to ourselves that we almost never want.

Then, of course, there's always a possibility of rejection when you're talking about eye contact. If you seek to make eye contact with someone and yet they refuse it, it can lead to a spiral of negative thoughts about reasons it happened.

Eye contact is *putting yourself out there* in a minor sense, and every time that happens, rejection is a possibility.

Attempt to focus.

If you're not practiced or not used to it, eye contact can take a good amount of your mental resources to hold.

Initially, it's a mental juggle to do two things at once – speak or listen, and hold eye contact. It's almost like rubbing your stomach in a circle and patting your head at once. It can be distracting and impossible for some.

When we want to convey something with precision, especially more in-depth and serious points, sometimes we eschew eye contact to save our mental resources for the words themselves.

Sometimes lacking eye contact can be functional. You just don't want to forget what you're talking about.

Hiding.

The final common reason that people avoid eye contact or are bad at it is because they want to hide something... but not in a deceiving sense.

It's been disproven many times that the lack of eye contact is not an accurate indicator of truthfulness and honesty.

Yet it's undeniable that it's more difficult to make eye contact with people when we are more emotional. There can be a sense of too much vulnerability, which for some people is just a stone's throw away from insecurity and self-doubt.

So reducing eye contact when we are otherwise vulnerable is hiding and protecting yourself in a sense. It just feels more stable and secure.

Superhuman eye contact, as you can see, is mostly difficult for reasons of security.

Chapter 3. Okay, so what IS superhuman eye contact?

I'm actually not going to give you a role model to aspire to for a couple of reasons.

First, there are actually no public figures that demonstrate it in a meaningful way, at least that has been captured on film or camera.

Anything that might be seen as a good example is probably too unnatural for us to emulate, and this book is all about real eye contact that you can use.

Second, pointing to someone puts a mental image in your head of someone to emulate, and this style might not be compatible with yours at all.

In other words, it won't be you. It will be forced and awkward, and you will literally be attempting to perform a pale imitation of someone else, which isn't a recipe for success. It's far more effective to internalize guidelines, and then create your own version of superhuman eye contact.

After all, the best eye contact is just the type that works for you and that you will commit to.

For the record, bad, subhuman, or even zombie eye contact is far easier to give an example for because there are very clear things you should avoid.

You should avoid the intense and unblinking eye contact that a television news anchor makes with the camera is bad. More eye contact is not better; don't mistake the two. There is a big difference from staring at someone's eyes and gazing deep into them.

Have you ever try to stare into someone's eyes like that? They'll think you are trying to violate their soul and withdraw accordingly. When you never break eye contact, it creates an uncomfortable tension.

Eye contact tension ranges from acceptable, good, and even seductive... but only if you remain within a certain range – if you hold it above and below a certain length of time. If you hold it too long, the tension rises into "creepy" territory.

Okay, so what constitutes superhuman eye contact?

It's constant but not unrelenting and invasive.

It's expressive and not devoid of emotion.

It's strong but not overpowering.

It gives the impression of empathy and full attention.

It's engaging and approachable.

Finally, it creates an appropriate amount of tension.

You may not find this very description very helpful right now, but I promise you it will become far clearer after the next chapter.

Chapter 4. Eye contact BOOT CAMP!

Welcome to eye contact boot camp, where the good become great, and the great become *superhuman* at eye contact.

This chapter is what I would consider the meat of the book because it contains many contact tips and tricks I've picked up over my years of coaching eye contact and charisma. I combined tips from my coaching practice, courses I've created, and good old scientific studies.

Included with most pieces of advice is an exercise that is designed to strengthen and improve that particular aspect of eye contact.

I hope that you see through this chapter that gaining superhuman eye contact is truly something that can be trained and gained, and isn't an immutable quality that some people were just lucky to be born with.

It's important to remember that not every piece of advice resonates with everyone, as each of us interacts with others in different ways.

The vast majority of the tips will universally improve your eye contact, but endless factors dictate how they will fit into our lives, such as:

- Personality
- Speech cadence and rhythm
- Speech patterns
- Amount of gesticulation
- Sense of humor
- The message you want to convey
- Cultural differences

In the end, just remember that the tips and exercises that you'll actually use – those are the best ways to improve your eye contact.

Superhuman Eye Contact Tip #1: Increase your tension tolerance.

When we think about the actual mechanics of great eye contact, it's not that difficult.

As I stated before, most of the time it's enough to just not be terrible at eye contact and you're in. Showing up is truly half the battle with eye contact.

The mechanics are simple but it's much easier said than done.

Why is that?

It's simply because the tension of holding eye contact is too great for you.

You're not used to it, you become alarmed and panic, and you break it. You know the feeling – it's like the other person's eyes start boring into your head.

For some of us, our tension tolerance is quite high. Personally, I feel comfortable not breaking eye contact for hours – of course, that would make me look like a maniac.

But for many others, tension tolerance is a mere millisecond. That is, you start feeling tension in your eyes and have to break eye contact in less than a second.

This tip is about realizing exactly what's keeping you from the strong, powerful eye contact you want. You need to increase the amount of tension you can tolerate from eye contact and the rest of the story will be a snap.

How does this make other people feel?

Actually, it's more important to talk about how the lack of tension tolerance makes others feel. It makes them feel uncomfortable and judgmental – in that they will judge you to be untrustworthy and preoccupied if you can't meet their gaze for more than 1-2 seconds.

Tension tolerance is one of the cornerstones of eye contact because if you can't resist the urge to look away, the rest of the advice in this book will be for naught.

<u>Exercise.</u>

Tension tolerance is all about exposure and practice. The more exposure to eye contact tension, the more you can tolerate it and eventually build up to the level you desire.

But where do you start? Like a baby learning to waddle.

First, you make eye contact and literally hold eye contact with people on television. Many of you might want to skip this step, but before you do, give it a quick try with a television news anchor. News anchors by nature stare directly at the camera and don't break eye contact because their teleprompter is right in front of the camera. This means that you will get the chance to hold a gaze that never breaks and get used to the tension there.

By the way, guess why the teleprompters are right over the camera? So that the news anchors can maintain eye contact and appear more trustworthy and honest!

The next step in increasing your tension tolerance is to stare at your own eyes in the mirror. This is actually more difficult than it sounds. Try it for a period of 30 seconds first, and talk to yourself in the mirror. Is it easy?

You are still going to get that feeling of tension, even with yourself. Resist the urge to look away and fight through the way your eyes start feeling like lead weights.

The more uncomfortable staring at your own eyes in the mirror is, the more you have to increase your tension tolerance.

The final step is to bring the fight to real people. What you are going to do is grab a pair of sunglasses and walk outside to an area with plenty of foot traffic. Place yourself in the path of the foot traffic, where you will be facing people walking by.

Put your sunglasses on and simply stare at people's eyes as they walk by. Remember, they can't see your eyes, so you should feel fearless in doing this.

Stare at people with impunity!

Notice how even though they don't think you're looking at them, they won't make prolonged eye contact with you. Train yourself to experience the full effects of tension, yet behind the safe walls of your sunglasses. You're exposing yourself fully to live eye contact but without a chance of embarrassment or rejection. Try to do this for 5 minutes a day for a week straight, and then notice how much more confidence you are with eye contact.

Of course, once you feel comfortable with sunglasses, the next step is to remove them completely. Make eye contact with everyone walking by you and get used to the tension.

Pretend you are playing a game called "eyes" and the winner is decided by how many seconds of eye contact he can achieve in the least time.

Your tension tolerance should be the last thing preventing superhuman eye contact, so let's make it bulletproof.

Superhuman Eye Contact Tip #2: Use the 80% and 50% ratios.

I've talked about ratios in conversation quite a bit before, and it's surprising how simply keeping track of how much you are talking can make a difference in how people perceive you.

[For those that haven't read any of my other books, I recommend going into conversation with a rough 2:1 ratio of questions asked:personal interjections. In other words, for every two questions you ask someone, you should talk about yourself once. It's a technique that gives your conversation partner the spotlight they usually crave, but also allows you to share your life.]

I found a way to integrate numbers into conversation, and I've also found a way to integrate numbers into eye contact.

<u>Here's part one of the bottom line</u>: When someone is talking to you, make eye contact 80% of the time.

In other words, keep their gaze and continue to look at their face while you are listening. Don't look around the room and behind them; it's distracting and gives the impression that you aren't listening.

If you keep looking at them, it simply makes you look attentive and like you care what they are talking about. The 20% where you aren't making eye contact is important because in the same vein, staring at someone 100% of the time makes you appear to be zoning out and not listening. So let people feel heard and validated by maintaining eye contact with them 80% of the time when they are speaking.

<u>Bottom line part two</u>: When you are speaking to someone, make eye contact with them 50% of the time.

When speaking, you'll notice that it's incredibly difficult to make eye contact a majority of the time. It's because holding eye contact requires a certain percentage of your mental faculties, so when you hold eye contact, it will probably cause your train of thought to derail a bit.

But holding 100% eye contact when you're speaking is also a bit unnerving and makes it appear that you are lecturing or preaching to someone. Chances are that you're not a professor speaking to his class, so maintaining this kind of eye contact while speaking is highly uncomfortable for the listener.

If you've never noticed, it's downright odd to have someone staring you in the eye while speaking to you.

If you stare at someone while you speak, you don't allow them to react as they would naturally. You put a spotlight on them inadvertently that makes them feel pressure to react to your eye contact and words in a certain way.

Maintaining a 50% ratio when you speak gives the listener freedom to process your words as they please, and also allows you focus on your words instead of eye contact.

Keep in mind that this is a rough but helpful guideline. If you find yourself highly off-base from either of these figures, it's time to reevaluate!

How does this make other people feel?

Relieved and comfortable. When they are speaking, they'll know that you are listening to them, which increases how much they enjoy speaking to you. It puts them at ease and doesn't make them feel judged.

When others are listening, you give them space to act how they want and not put on a series of fake laughs for your sake. You give enough eye contact to be engaging, but not enough to be unnerving.

Superhuman Eye Contact Tip #3: Decrease the amount of tension felt.

Superhuman Eye Contact Tip #1 was focused on increasing the amount of tolerance you have for eye contact tension.

But there are two ways to deal with a given amount of tension: by increasing your tolerance for it, or by decreasing the amount that the tension affects you.

This tip focuses on the latter.

Decreasing the amount that tension affects you is all a matter of perspective.

Eye contact tension will always be there, but if you can distract yourself from the elephant in the room, it makes eye contact almost too easy.

Tension exists mainly because we think about it and are unable to forget about it. The instant that you become distracted or focused on something else, tension disappears and you can focus on the task at hand.

We see this in all other walks of life.

If you want a baby to eat his vegetables, you pretend the spoon is an airplane coming in for a crash landing in the hangar. If you want to fly on an airplane without freaking out, you might distract yourself with alcohol.

If you want to improve a conversation, pretend that you're a talk show host and are interviewing your conversation partner. And so on.

If you can distract yourself similarly with eye contact, you can easily decrease the tension you feel.

Here are a few ways you can distract yourself from the tension:

- Try to determine exactly what color their eyes are?
- Figure out which planet their eyes resemble the most?

- Count how many veins they have in the whites of their eyes?
- Determine which sunglasses shape would best fit their eye and face shape?
- You get the idea.

How does this make other people feel?

When you distract yourself, you become far more comfortable with eye contact. And if you distract yourself with any of the tactics listed above, you also appear more interested and engaged than you would otherwise.

So people will feel that you're a great captive audience that is comfortable with the interaction.

Exercise.

This is a technique that is fairly amazing at decreasing the tension you feel.

Take a chair and seat yourself right in front of the wall, maybe four feet away. Preferably, you'd be sitting in front of a poster – something with a focal point or something in particular to stare at. Ideally something with a face.

First stare at the face. Shift the focus of your sight to your peripherals, but leave your eyes 100% on the face.

In other words, think about when you are checking out someone of the opposite sex. You appear to be looking at your friend, but in reality, you are focusing on them through your peripheral vision.

The end result is that you appear to be engaged and making eye contact with your friend or whoever is in front of you, but your focus is elsewhere. This means that there is literally almost no eye contact tension felt... because you aren't really looking at them! Your eyes appear to be, but your mind is occupied elsewhere.

Practice sitting in front of the wall and leaving your eyes primarily on the wall, but attempt to focus on things in your peripheral vision such as furniture, other posters, or people.

The best way to decrease the eye contact felt is to mentally not even make eye contact!

Superhuman Eye Contact Tip #4: Stay in the eye contact triangle.

Now that you're hopefully a bit more practiced and comfortable with eye contact tension, we can get into a bit more advanced techniques.

We know that we shouldn't keep holding eye contact because that makes you appear like a zombie, and people typically aren't comfortable with staring zombies.

Staring endlessly is a huge red flag that someone isn't listening or seeing the social cues I'm dropping. I'd even go as far to say that I assume that starers typically have lower social and emotional intelligence. As I mentioned before, there is a world of difference between staring at someone's eyes and gazing deeply into them.

Breaking eye contact occasionally is essential to great eye contact, as weird as it sounds.

But how long and how should one break eye contact? These are the mechanical questions that actually matter.

I'll address each in order.

How long should I actually maintain eye contact?

Use 5 seconds as a guideline. Maintain strong eye contact without wavering... and then glance away to break it every 5 seconds.

It's because 5 seconds is the sweet spot – any longer than 5 seconds and your eye contact starts turning into an unnerving stare, any shorter and your eye contact isn't engaging or attentive.

It also prevents you from turning into a zombie that ignores all other signs a person is putting out. Breaking eye contact every 5 seconds will help you become more observant and attuned to people's social cues.

How should I break eye contact?

When breaking eye contact, there are better ways to do it than to look at your watch or pretend to cough. Those of course work, but there are optimal ways to break eye contact.

The best way to do so is to stay in the triangle of the right eye, left eye, and point of the nose.

So every 5 seconds, you will take your eyes on a journey – clockwise or counter, it doesn't matter – through the facial triangle. Have the journey last at last a couple of seconds, but don't rush it otherwise you will look like you are having some sort of eye seizure.

Take your eyes through the triangle and end up back at the eyes.

You can also choose to focus on one eye in particular for 5 seconds, go through the triangle, then end up on the other eye for 5 seconds. You can also do the same with focusing on the nose for 5 seconds.

There are endless combinations you can use in the context of the eye contact triangle. What matters is that you break eye contact and then change the position of focus every 5 seconds.

Staying in the triangle works well with eye contact because it relieves the building tension of prolonged eye contact, but it also keeps you appearing attentive. After all, if someone is scanning your face, it surely gives the impression of engagement and interest.

The only downside of the eye contact triangle is that it absolutely requires practice – on two levels.

First, tracing your eyes through the triangle is harder than you might expect at first. Eyes biologically cannot smoothly slide from one location to the next, so you must practice having your eyes move in the triangle as slowly as possible.

Second, it requires you to have a clock inside your head addressing all of this, which is counterproductive because it requires you to do two things at once and hampers your listening ability. After a critical mass of practice, you will begin to internalize how often you need to break eye contact.

Another way to break eye contact is to squint one or both of your eyes.

Squinting and narrowing your eyes at someone while maintaining eye contact cuts off all the tension that previously existed and essentially resets the clock. I mean squinting like you might do when you are thinking hard about something or trying to figure something out. It's another effective way of breaking eye contact while appearing engaged – you literally look like you are thinking hard about what they have just said.

How does this make other people feel?

Supremely comfortable. That they are being listened to by someone with high emotional intelligence.

This is the stage when people will begin to label you as someone with amazing eye contact. When you can navigate it at this level, you will put people at ease and make them feel like you've been a friend for many years. These feelings of closeness and intimacy are what superhuman eye contact can create.

The eye contact triangle does require practice, however, so initially you might make other people feel... confused.

Superhuman Eye Contact Tip #5: No zombie eyes.

One of the biggest problems with eye contact is that people have the wrong perception of what constitutes good eye contact.

This frequently results in what I like to call zombie eyes.

A zombie is a creature who used to be a person. They have died, and the zombie has risen in their place. They are undead and don't seem to have the ability for any type of meaningful thought beyond "I'm hungry, that living creature seems pretty tasty."

Zombie eyes are dead eyes.

Eyes that show no emotion and no evidence of a train of thought.

This frequently happens because most people equate the amount of eye contact with its strength. In other words, the more eye contact, the better, despite the fact that in reality eye contact above a certain amount makes people supremely uncomfortable.

Zombie eyes are when someone makes eye contact with you and just stares. It's almost as if they don't even blink, they're just so intent on staring into your soul. They are expressionless and unflinching. I get uncomfortable just thinking about it.

The best way to combat zombie eyes is to actively show emotion through your eyes and eyebrows.

Most people don't intend to have perpetual poker faces and zombie eyes, we just aren't aware of the non-verbal messages we are or aren't sending.

For example, when you watch a comedy or horror movie alone, perhaps you don't show any emotion on your face because no one is around to react to it. But does your face actually change when people are around and depending on it for an emotional reaction? Make sure it does, otherwise other people have probably branded you as someone with zombie eyes.

When you defeat zombie eyes and emote through your eye contact, you will be able to express thoughts and feelings without having to say a word. Otherwise, you may come off as the physical embodiment of a monotone.

How does this make other people feel?

Zombie eyes make people feel extremely self-conscious and defensive.

When someone stares at your mouth too long, you feel like you might have something stuck in your teeth. It's the same with eye contact that doesn't show any emotion – *is there something wrong with me, did I say something wrong, or are you angry about something*?

On top of it all, it makes people feel unheard and like there is something slightly off about you.

Emotional reactance is a huge part of conversation, and if your eyes aren't consistent with the conversation's content, you will appear inconsistent... as liars and untrustworthy people do.

How would it make you feel if you just had a child and were excitedly telling someone, and yet their eye contact was just a blank stare?

<u>Exercise.</u>

Unlike some other aspects of eye contact, zombie eyes can be a true awareness problem. If people aren't aware of how they appear or are non-verbally acting, it's something that can be corrected with a bit of practice.

There's a two-part exercise I like to recommend in correcting zombie eyes and really getting better at showing emotion non-verbally through the eyes.

The first part you can do by yourself.

If you're aware that you are poor at showing emotion and expressing yourself with your facial expressions, the first step is to evaluate just how bad you are. You are going to put the television on and sit in front of a mirror. Put on a comedy show, or something that will make you react visibly in some way. Horror also works well because of the visceral emotional reactions it commands.

Face the mirror, not the television. Listen to the television show and with only your facial expressions, demonstrate the emotions of the words that are said on the television.

Are you expressing what you thought you were with your face? You will be able to evaluate just how expressive your face and eyes are, as well as see how much you need to ramp it up. If it feels like you're exaggerating everything just to convey an emotion with your face, you probably need a good bit of practice to defeat your inner zombie eyes.

The next step of this exercise requires a friend who is aware of the exercise. You are going to have a normal conversation with them, except one thing – you can't talk.

You're a mute. You have to demonstrate your responses and emotional reactions non-verbally and only with your facial expressions and eyes. This will teach you how much effort you need to put into expression and let you practice it in a safe space.

Numerous studies have confirmed the fact that non-verbal communication is far more important than words. Take this to heart and destroy your zombie eyes.

Superhuman Eye Contact Tip #6: Approach from the side.

Aside from being a social interaction and conversation specialist, I am also a dating coach. The three go hand-in-hand and are sometimes the exact same lesson but from different angles.

Date coaching is all about teaching the delicate dance of putting forth signs of interest in a measured and confident manner. Too much interest and you are giving yourself away, too little interest and you have failed to assert yourself.

That's a massive oversimplification, but the reason I bring it up is because it's the same with eye contact. You simply can't go in too strong and intense with it or you'll scare off the person you're trying to talk to.

That brings me to the title of this chapter: approach from the side.

Being that eye contact is a direct and confrontational thing, as I discussed in the beginning in this book, it's something that must be given out carefully at times. You have to remember that even though you've improved your eye contact talents, most people do not take such initiative in self-development – especially something they might not realize the true value of like eye contact.

The majority of people you will encounter during your day are going to be bad at eye contact.

Remember how it was when you were bad it? You would get intimidated, scared, and flustered when someone made strong eye contact with you. It felt like they were violating you because you simply didn't know how to deal with it.

You need to approach from the side with eye contact!

What I mean by this is that prolonged eye contact when you are face-to-face in front of someone can be very intense for some people.

Just this alone can cause them to turn red in the face and develop sweaty palms. It's essentially a low-grade personal space violation if you're in front of them because they are so open and vulnerable to you.

So instead of pairing face-to-face interaction + strong eye contact, stand at people's side or from a larger distance. Let them feel like their personal space is still completely intact, and they will be more comfortable with your strong eye contact and feel less of a need to defend themselves and disengage.

Is it really that big of a deal? Well, yes.

It is a big deal because you don't ever want to make someone feel uncomfortable, especially with eye contact. If you can sense that someone might be uncomfortable, approaching from the side or even just breaking eye contact every 2-3 seconds might be the difference in them opening up to you at all.

This lesson about approaching from the side sheds light on a couple of things.

First, everyone has their own struggles, and you might actually be in the position of power when it comes to eye contact. Keep an eye out for this and make sure that you aren't going to intimidate them in any way.

Second, there truly is a thing as too much eye contact. Eye contact inherently is direct and inquisitive, and if you happen upon someone who isn't comfortable with either of those things, they will recoil. You need to adjust to the person.

Each of us has a certain amount of tolerance for personal space invasion. For some, you could have your hands in their pockets and they wouldn't care… but for others, simple eye contact face-to-face would be too much. You have to adapt and calibrate to everyone's tolerance level, and you can compensate for strong eye contact by giving them additional physical space.

For further illustration, let's think about why Catholic confessionals and couches in psychiatrist offices are constructed to reduce the amount of eye contact between the involved parties. Or why it's hard to look at someone in the eye when you are making an emotional or intimate observation. Eye contact is a huge aspect of personal space, and if you feel that you are baring yourself in other ways, reducing the amount of eye contact can help compensate.

In summation, avoid eye contact with people that you know need the space.

How does this make other people feel?

Relieved.

Just imagine the following scenario (and it's probably easy for you because you were once bad with eye contact).

The life of the party comes to talk to you and they make incessant and constant eye contact with you. They're right in front of you, inching closer, and not giving you a chance to gather your thoughts because you can only focus on the lack of personal space you have. And their eyes, you can't avoid them very well so you just stare dumbfounded...

Allowing people the chance to avoid that scenario is quite relieving indeed.

Superhuman Eye Contact Tip #7: Practice at Chili's.

A lot of the eye contact tips in this book may seem like good ideas, but how can you truly practice them and begin to internalize them without looking like a maniac?

Thankfully, there are people whose job it literally is to be nice to you and deal with you.

I'm talking of course about the waiters and waitresses that serve you at restaurants such as Chili's.

Normally I would say cashiers and baristas and the like, but they're so focused on so many different things for their job that they can't devote that much time to you. Servers, however, always have time to read you the special of the day, so they are much better practice partners for eye contact.

Servers are paid to be nice to you, so there's literally no downside to trying any of the eye contact tips in this book and failing. If you fail, so what? You may not even be able to tell because they'll just laugh it off and bring your shrimp cocktail.

You should view them as great guinea pigs to test out your new jokes and new eye contact skills on. A major reason that we don't often venture out of our comfort zones is because we don't know just how bad an ensuing failure will be. Our imagination runs wild with negative thoughts.

Most of the time, it's fairly negligible. An awkward laugh and you move on... but it's still something that we have to discover for ourselves to truly get over.

With servers as guinea pigs, you get to experience the eye contact successes that will build up your confidence, and transfer them to your social life. You also get to experience the inevitable eye contact failures in a safe space, where you will learn that the worst case scenario really isn't so bad.

A slightly awkward moment that no one will remember later? I'll take that any day.

A final benefit to practicing your eye contact with servers is you'll get to interact with people who likely have great eye contact! Servers are nothing if not people-oriented, so they probably have developed a good sense of eye contact and conversational intelligence. Short banter and witty remarks are their daily currency, so practicing with them is an excellent baseline to start with.

You can practice increasing your tension tolerance by simply staring them in the eye. You can literally count your 80% and 50% ratios out loud while talking to them to get accustomed to how they feel.

You can decrease the amount of tension by deciding that you simply need to discover their eye color. You can practice destroying your zombie eyes by speaking as little as possible and emoting through your facial expressions. And so on.

Just don't ask them about their flair.

Superhuman Eye Contact Tip #8: Eye strength for eye contact.

Lost in the shuffle about eye contact and it's various virtues is the simple fact that eye contact depends on the eyes, which are held in place by muscles.

If you want to get better at something that ultimately depends on a set of muscles, it only makes sense that you should strengthen the underlying muscles themselves.

At a certain point, most physical acts are like riding a bike.

Once you recognize the feeling of the action and understand how to generate it, it's encased in your muscles for all eternity – you don't really forget it. You might get rusty, but you will have a perpetual baseline of ability and performance.

If you can develop the muscles to a certain threshold of strength, as well as set in stone a sense of muscle memory, then sometimes it won't matter how nervous or anxious you are about eye contact. It will be instinct.

Put more simply, strong eyes help strong eye contact.

When you think about it, our natural eye contact is probably at its weakest point right now in the history of human civilization. We have computers, technology, and the impending Terminator-like destruction of society to thank for this.

Our ocular muscles are so weak because the majority of us spend massive amounts of time staring at digital screens like laptops and kindles (ahem...).

Now that we know that weak eye muscles are a large cause of weak eye contact, let's dive into some exercises to strengthen them. Some have actually postulated that these exercises can improve your sight as well, but I won't go that far.

The figure 8.

The figure 8 is when you trace the number 8 with your eyes.

To spell it out, you look left, left-up, center, down-right, right, up-right, center, down-left, left... and so on. Hold at each position for 1 second then move on. Do this every other day at first, for 10 rounds. You can adjust accordingly when your eyes get stronger.

When you're looking left, stretch as far left as your eyes can go. Do this same stretch for every direction that you look in for the figure 8. Use the center as a resting point to give your eyes a short respite. The important part of this exercise is to stretch the range of your eyes. This prevents zombie eyes and automatically makes your eyes more expressive if they have a larger range.

The pirate.

Pirates often have eye patches, so this was a natural name for this exercise.

All of us have a dominant eye, and in some cases, it's very apparent. Not only is this a bit odd visually, it means that your non-dominant eye is passive and doesn't participate in eye contact very well.

The task of the day is to strengthen your non-dominant eye. The way that optometrists do this is to literally give you an eyepatch for a period of time so that you force the non-dominant eye to take charge and not allow it to be compensated for.

We will do something similar. You are simply going to cover your eyes, one at a time. Use your hand.

Then you are simply going to look up, down, left, and right (in this order) and hold for 1 second in each direction. Like with the figure 8, you are going to stretch as far as you can in each respective direction. When you do this one eye at a time, it strengthens your non-dominant eye.

This will actually feel quite odd in your non-dominant eye at first because it is so unused to focusing on its own. Embrace this as a sign of imminent progress!

Zooming.

Eye contact occurs in a range of distances. The farther you are, the easier it is, but the less effective and powerful it is. Of course, the closer you are in proximity to someone else's

eyes, the larger an effect the eye contact has...
and, of course, the harder it is to hold.

In fact, once you investigate it more, it's quite
hard to hold your eye focus on something that
is close to your face, person or not. That's why
this exercise is so important. It's useful for
everything in your life, not just eye contact.

Here's what you do.

You reach your arm out so that your elbow is
straight and stick your thumb up. Focus on
your thumb.

Slowly bring your thumb closer to your face,
focusing on it the entire time. Stop when the
thumb is about 4 inches away from your face.
Wait for your eyes to focus on the thumb and
hold it there for 3 seconds.

Then move your thumb slowly away until your
arm is straight again. Repeat this a few times a
day. You can also do this one eye at a time,
which I would recommend doing after a few
days of doing it with both eyes.

You get to strengthen your eye through the
entire range of distances that it will focus on
throughout the day. No longer get eye fatigue
when holding eye contact for extended periods

of time, or when you're in closer quarters with someone. Treat the eye like any other muscle and warm it up and condition it and it will perform better for your purposes.

Superhuman Eye Contact Tip #9: Sometimes you *want* tension...

I mentioned before that eye contact should induce the appropriate amount of tension for each context.

For most contexts, the appropriate amount of tension is very small, possibly none. You actually want to be building as much comfort as possible, and tension is essentially the opposite of that.

There are essentially two types of interaction as far as eye contact is concerned, ones that build comfort and rapport and ones to create tension.

Interactions for comfort and rapport are what you typically want to focus on on a daily basis.

Meeting new people, talking to co-workers, and hanging out at a barbecue are where comfort and rapport reign supreme. These will be probably 90% of your interactions, and that's why this book is focused on increasing your tension tolerance and decreasing the amount of tension you feel.

Interactions for tension are where tension is arousing and desirable as opposed to uncomfortable. Of course, I'm talking primarily about flirtation and interactions with the opposite sex.

Tension can be sexy sometimes!

It's the feeling where your heart drops to your stomach, it flutters, and makes you sweat all over. Tension is one of the huge drivers of human attraction and sexuality, and resolving that tension is often a motivator for all things dating.

So there are two distinctly different types of tension. How can you go about generating the kind that makes someone's heart beat out of their chest?

It's in the delivery. Remember that more eye contact is not necessarily better, so it's all about being intentional with the amount of eye contact that you do utilize.

Tell me how, already!

Stickiness.

Ever hear the term "sticky eyes"?

Sticky eyes are one of the best ways, hands down, to impart the feeling of sexual tension. The name comes from the fact that you should act like your eyes have glue running to the other person's eyes.

This means that when you look away from their eyes and break eye contact, your eyes should linger on theirs, even after you start turning your head. Let the strand of glue keep your eyes on theirs long after it would normally end, like you can't look away from them. Give them the impression that you are reluctant to look away at all.

Every time you make eye contact, imagine that you are giving them a look that says "I want to take you dancing in the moonlight."

Your eye contact motions are slow and intentional, and there are no quick movements. Even your blinks are deliberate and slow. You don't flick your eyes to the side like you usually would, and you don't scan the room or their face quickly like you would with other people. You don't react to small things and let them interrupt your gaze.

It's like nothing can drag you away from their eyes.

Sticky eyes are pretty much the epitome of bedroom eyes. Bedroom eyes are seductive, intense, and inquisitive.

It's not the quantity but the quality of eye contact here. Sticky eyes create anticipation.

How does this make other people feel?

Well, it depends on how they feel about you. If they don't like you or aren't interested in you that way, they might feel uncomfortable.

If they like you, they will be able to sense that you are interested in them. Sticky eyes are a very strong indicator or romantic interest, and locking eyes like that can be very arousing.

You will make them feel turned on and slightly self-conscious, but not in a negative way – self-conscious in the way that you are appreciating them and they are recognizing it.

Superhuman Eye Contact Tip #10: Direction matters.

Despite the proven advice in this book, one thing you cannot account for is people's differences.

You can do everything exactly right and still give too much or too little eye contact for people based on their preferences or upbringing.

Some people like baseball and some people like politics. The exact reasons for this preference are infinite.

If someone was raised in a conservative household, they might feel that any amount of eye contact is invasive and highly suggestive. The only eye contact they got when they were young was when they were being scolded by their parents. How does this influence them to this day?

Or if someone was repeatedly told that eye contact was a sign of respect and glancing away for a second was akin to a dog showing his soft underbelly. How might they approach eye contact differently?

So people are different. You'll have to adapt your eye contact skills and tension to the person you're talking to.

But studies have actually shown that there are patterns you can see in eye movements that are consistent among a majority of people.

Lateral eye movements (LEMs).

If you're in the midst of an eye contact-heavy conversation with someone, the direction they look when they break the eye contact can be heavily indicative of what is going on inside of their head.

While it's impossible to literally read people's minds, several extremely consistent thought patterns have been discovered from LEMs. In other words, the way people look when they are talking has incredible predictive power in what people are thinking.

More confirmation for these findings is the fact that consistent patterns have emerged in right-handed people, and the patterns are essentially reversed in left-handed people.

The interesting part is this implies that LEMs are hemispheric by nature, which lends support to theories about left-brain and right-brain functionality.

Right-brain dominant people tend to tout themselves are more creative, free-flowing, and expressive. They are the artists of the world.

Left-brain dominant people tend to be characterized as logical, stern, and concrete. They are the proverbial and literal bankers of the world.

So what LEMs indicate?

For a right-handed person:

- If they look right
    - And up, they are accessing constructed imagery, which you can interpret as a lie or made up image.
    - To the side, and they are constructing sounds and words,

which you can interpret as a lie or made up speech.

- o And down, and they are accessing tactile and visceral feelings, which you can generally interpret to be genuine and true.
- If they look left
  - o And up, they are accessing remembered imagery, which you can interpret as a true and genuine memory.
  - o To the side, they are accessing remembered sounds and words, which you can interpret as recollections of real conversations.
  - o And down, they are accessing sensory information, which you can interpret as observational and true.
- If they look straight on with an unfocused gaze, they are quickly accessing sensory information, which you can interpret as true and genuine observations about how they currently feel.

Remember that these patterns are reversed in left-handed people, and often mixed in ambidextrous people.

What does this mean for you in practical terms? It means that you have a good chance

of lie detection based on how people break
their eye contact!

It turns out that the saying that "eyes are the
window to the soul" was close, but needs a
slight adjustment. It appears that "how one
breaks eye contact is the window to the soul" is
somewhat more accurate.

Conclusion

Being told that the way I came off to others — essentially how likable I was — was a big blow to my ego.

It might have been for the best, however, that I learned my lesson with such low stakes like a summer internship, and relatively early in life as opposed to plodding through life alienating people left and right.

It's like the military bootcamp process — they break you down to nothing so that they can rebuild you the correct way.

Also like the military, eye contact was something that I had to drill myself into comfort with. It's unnatural to look people in the eye so directly and strong — in the wild, that's an invitation to having a hyena tear your throat out.

It's a human social construct that we've come to associate with positive traits, so heres's an idea – becoming superhuman at it will associate you with amazing traits.

In the end, eye contact is only a component of an amazing presence and impression, but improving your eye contact will open doors for you.

You've probably never thought about eye contact in such depth before this book, and it might be a little bit overwhelming. But persevere and practice. Remember how many times you had to fall to ride your bike? It's a process that will become second nature very quickly, and it's something that you can take throughout your life.

Sincerely,

Patrick King
The Social Interaction Specialist
www.PatrickKingConsulting.com

P.S. If you enjoyed this book, please don't be shy and drop me a line, leave a review, or both! I love reading feedback, and reviews are the lifeblood of Kindle books, so they are always welcome and greatly appreciated.

Other books by Patrick King include:

CHATTER: Small Talk, Charisma, and How to Talk to Anyone

MAGNETIC: How to Impress, Connect, and Influence

The Science of Likability: Charm, Wit, Humor, and the 16 Studies That Show You How To Master Them

Cheat Sheet

Chapter 1. Why is eye contact so important?

Because it's a prerequisite. If you don't have at least decent eye contact, you'll be assumed to have the worst of traits and intentions. If you have superhuman eye contact, you'll be assumed to have the best of traits. Why not capitalize?

Chapter 2. Why is superhuman eye contact so difficult?

A combination of the lack of directness in our daily lives, combined with unawareness and anxiety contribute to most people's eye contact being shifty and weak.

Chapter 3. Okay, so what IS superhuman eye contact?

Superhuman eye contact is a balance, and ultimately makes the other person feel comfortable with you. Don't forget, that is the overarching goal.

Superhuman Eye Contact Tip #1: Increase your tension tolerance.

The biggest factor that prevents us from improving our eye contact is our inability to tolerate the tension that eye contact creates. Thus, drilling tension tolerance with exposure exercises will make the rest of this book more useful.

Superhuman Eye Contact Tip #2: Use the 80% and 50% ratios.

When someone is speaking to you, maintain eye contact with them 80% of the time to appear attentive and engaged. When you are speaking to others, maintain eye contact 50% of the time to appear thoughtful and interested.

Superhuman Eye Contact Tip #3: Decrease the amount of tension felt.

To deal with the inevitable eye contact tension, you can also simply decrease how much you feel it by distracting yourself with questions about their eyes and face.

Superhuman Eye Contact Tip #4: Stay in the eye contact triangle.

When you break eye contact, you don't need to break it by looking off to the side. You can break it by staying on the other person's face if you stay within the right eye, left eye, and tip of the nose.

Superhuman Eye Contact Tip #5: No zombie eyes.

Zombie eyes are expressionless and emotionless. Make sure that you are showing some type of emotion through your eyes and eyebrows when you make eye contact, otherwise you are closer to a creepy stare.

Superhuman Eye Contact Tip #6: Approach from the side.

People have varying degrees of comfort with personal space violations. Eye contact is inherently a personal space violation, so you need to adjust the amount you use based on how invasive you are physically, mentally, or emotionally.

Superhuman Eye Contact Tip #7: Practice at Chili's.

Servers are great people to practice eye contact with because it is literally their job to be nice to you. In addition, you learn to build confidence with small eye contact successes.

Superhuman Eye Contact Tip #8: Eye strength for eye contact.

Eye contact is powered by the ocular muscles, so it only makes sense that you exercise your ocular muscles and eventually develop a sense of muscle memory regarding eye contact.

Superhuman Eye Contact Tip #9: Sometimes you *want* tension...

Most of the time you want to decrease tension with your eye contact, but sometimes, notably when interacting and flirting with the opposite sex, you want to create a bit. You can do this with sticky eyes and giving them a different quality of eye contact, not quantity.

Superhuman Eye Contact Tip #10: Direction matters.

Studies have shown that the direction people look after breaking eye contact can be highly indicative as to whether they are thinking about lying or telling the truth. These directions are mirror images for right and left-handed people.

Made in the USA
San Bernardino, CA
14 January 2016